YOUR PASSPORT TO

ITALY

by Nancy Dickmann

CONTENT CONSULTANT

Professor Abigail Brundin

Faculty of Modern and Medieval Languages and Linguistics

University of Cambridge, UK

CAPSTONE PRESS

a capstone imprint

Capstone Captivate is published by Capstone Press, an imprint of Capstone.
1710 Roe Crest Drive
North Mankato, Minnesota 56003
www.capstonepub.com

Library of Congress Cataloging-in-Publication Data is available on the Library of Congress website.
ISBN: 978-1-4966-9551-2 (hardcover)
ISBN: 978-1-4966-9719-6 (paperback)
ISBN: 978-1-9771-5543-6 (eBook PDF)

Summary:
What would it be like to live in Italy? How is Italian culture unique? Explore the sights, traditions, and daily lives of people in Italy.

Image Credits
Capstone: Eric Gohl, 5; Getty Images: Shaun Botterill, 26; iStockphoto: Arghman, 18; Library of Congress: Prints and Photographs Division, 11; Shutterstock: Alexanderstock23, 24, Boris Stroujko, 13, DARRAY, 23, Davide Trolli, 9, gorillaimages, 29, kavram, 8, M. Rohana, 25, MikeDotta, 19, muratart, cover, Natursports, 15, StevanZZ, 7, Yaroslav Magistr, 16, YuliiaHolovchenko, 21

Design Elements
iStockphoto: Yevhenii Dubinko; Shutterstock: Filip Bjorkman, flipser, MicroOne, pingebat, sevenmoonlight

Editorial Credits
Editor: Clare Lewis; Designer: Juliette Peters,
Media Research: Tracy Cummins, Premedia: Laura Manthe

All internet sites appearing in back matter were available and accurate when this book was sent to press.

Printed and bound in the United States of America.   PO3837

CONTENTS

Words in **bold** are in the glossary.

CHAPTER ONE

WELCOME TO ITALY!

An ancient stone stadium sits in the middle of a bustling modern city. This is the Colosseum. It was built by the ancient Romans. It hosted **gladiator** games nearly 2,000 years ago. More than 7 million tourists still visit it each year.

Italy has many historic sites. The Colosseum is just one of them. Many are from the time of the Roman Empire. This **empire** once included parts of three continents. Today, Italy is the tenth largest country in Europe. Italy's landscape has many beautiful natural features. They include mountains, beaches, and rolling hills. Its busy cities are a mix of old and new. Italy is famous around the world for its food and fashion.

MAP OF ITALY

Explore Italy's cities and landmarks.

FACT FILE

OFFICIAL NAME: .... ITALIAN REPUBLIC
POPULATION: 62,402,659
LAND AREA: .... 113,568 SQ. MI. (294,140 SQ KM)
CAPITAL: .... ROME
MONEY: .... EURO
GOVERNMENT: .... PARLIAMENTARY REPUBLIC
LANGUAGE: .... ITALIAN
GEOGRAPHY:

Mainland Italy is a peninsula that extends into the central Mediterranean Sea. Its northern end borders France, Switzerland, Austria, and Slovenia. The large islands of Sardinia and Sicily are part of Italy.

NATURAL RESOURCES:

Italy's resources include coal, mercury, pumice, natural gas, crude oil, and fish.

CROSSROADS OF THE WORLD

The Italian **peninsula** is surrounded by the Mediterranean Sea. It has a long coastline. For many centuries, ships have visited its ports. Ports are harbor towns on the coast. These include the cities of Genoa and Naples. Traders came from around the world. They bought and sold goods such as silk and spices.

The Colosseum was officially opened by the emperor Titus in 80 CE.

Ships also brought people and ideas to Italy. It was known as a center for science and the arts. And it still is today! People from many countries now call Italy home. Many Italians have also settled in other countries. They have spread its culture.

CHAPTER TWO

HISTORY OF ITALY

Long ago, many small tribes lived in Italy. In the 700s BCE, a group called the Romans began to take over. They defeated neighboring tribes. Then they took over their land.

The Romans had a powerful army. They conquered lands outside Italy. By 117 CE, they ruled a huge area. The Romans built roads, bridges, and buildings. Many of them are still standing today.

The Pont du Gard in France was built by Romans after they had conquered France.

Michelangelo was one of the most famous artists of the Renaissance. He carved this sculpture.

THE RENAISSANCE

The Roman Empire ended in 476 CE. By about 1000 CE, Italy was divided into **city-states**. These had a main city that ruled over the area around it. Each city-state was **independent**.

In the 1300s, a period called the Renaissance began. It started in Italy. It soon spread to the rest of Europe. It was a time of great thinkers. They made scientific discoveries. They wrote poetry. They created paintings and sculptures.

A UNITED COUNTRY

After the Renaissance, Spain ruled most of Italy. Then France took over. But the Italians wanted to rule themselves. Some people wanted Italy's regions to join together. Fighting began in 1848. By 1871, Italy was united. It became an independent country.

WAR AND PEACE

In World War II, Italy joined forces with Germany. But they had to surrender to the **Allies** in 1943. After the war, the Italian people voted to become a **republic**. They would no longer have a king.

In 1958, Italy joined up with five other countries to make the European Economic Community. They wanted to work together. Other countries joined the group and it became the **European Union** in 1993.

FACT
Today, there are 27 countries in the European Union!

TIMELINE OF ITALIAN HISTORY

AROUND 753 BCE: The kingdom of Rome begins.

117 CE: The Roman Empire reaches its greatest size.

476: Rome is conquered and the Roman Empire ends.

1550s: Spain now rules most of Italy.

1796: French troops invade Italy and take over.

1861: The Kingdom of Italy is proclaimed, though it doesn't include Rome or Venice.

1871: All of Italy is unified into a single country.

1940: Italy joins World War II on the side of Germany.

1943: Italy surrenders to the Allies.

1946: The Italian people vote to form a republic, without a king.

1958: Italy joins the European Economic Community (EEC).

1993: The EEC becomes the European Union.

Giuseppe Garibaldi was a general who led the army that helped unite Italy in the 1860s.

CHAPTER THREE

EXPLORE ITALY

Italy is a popular country to explore. More than 60 million people visit each year. They come to see its historic sites and natural beauty. They also come for the food and culture.

BEAUTIFUL COASTLINES

Italy is in the south of Europe. Many parts of it are warm and sunny. People visit the sandy beaches on its long coastline. One of the most famous regions is the Amalfi Coast. It is south of Naples. Cliffs tower over the beaches. Many of them have villages perched at the top.

THE ITALIAN LAKES

In the north of Italy, there are beautiful lakes. They were carved out by ice thousands of years ago. The lakes are surrounded by beaches and towns. There are also mountains at the northern end. Ferries take tourists from town to town.

Positano is one of the most popular villages on the Amalfi Coast.

FACT

Lake Garda is the largest of the lakes, at 143 square miles (370 sq km). At 34 miles (54 km) long, Lake Maggiore is longer, but it is narrower.

MOUNTAINS

The Alps is Europe's largest mountain range. It stretches through the north of Italy and the surrounding countries. Many of the mountains are topped with snow all year round. The tallest, Mont Blanc (Monte Bianco in Italian), lies on Italy's border with France. People come to the Alps to ski and snowboard. Meadows and lakes lie between the jagged peaks.

VOLCANOES

Italy has several **volcanoes**. The most famous is probably Vesuvius. It looms over the city of Naples. Its last eruption was in 1944. Today, visitors can hike to the top. Mount Etna, in Sicily, erupts more often. So does Stromboli. This small island spews out lava almost constantly.

FACT

The Italian Alps are home to animals such as the chamois, which is a type of mountain goat. Chamois are good climbers. There are also marmots, which are related to groundhogs. They dig burrows in Alpine meadows. Visitors might also spot wolves or brown bears.

Stromboli's amazing nighttime eruptions have given it the nickname "the lighthouse of the Mediterranean."

Many tourists take a ride in a gondola to look at Venice's beautiful buildings.

EXCITING CITIES

Italy's cities have a long history. They have beautiful buildings and ancient sites. Rome is the capital of Italy. It is also one of the most popular cities to visit. Tourists come to see the Forum. It was the main plaza of the ancient city. The ruins of temples and public buildings are still visible.

Rome is a modern city too. It is full of cafés, restaurants, and shops. There is street art almost everywhere. Romans zoom around on scooters and motorcycles.

Venice is on the coast, in the north. It was built on small islands in a marshy lagoon. Instead of streets, there are **canals**. The only vehicles are boats. People walk along the narrow streets. There are 438 bridges connecting the islands.

POMPEII

The ancient Romans built the city of Pompeii. It was destroyed when Vesuvius erupted in 79 CE. The entire city was buried in ash. Archaeologists began to dig it out in the 1700s. The ash had preserved artifacts and buildings. Pompeii shows us what ancient Roman cities were like.

CHAPTER FOUR

DAILY LIFE

More than two-thirds of Italians live and work in cities. Most big cities are in the north. There are smaller towns and villages all over Italy. Many people in the countryside work on farms. They grow wheat, rice, tomatoes, olives, and grapes.

Many of Italy's olives are harvested and pressed to make olive oil.

18

SCHOOL

Children in Italy go to school in the mornings. There are lessons from 8:00 a.m. to 1:00 p.m. Then the children go home for lunch. On some days, they may stay in school for afternoon classes. Some schools are not open in the afternoons. These schools have classes on Saturday mornings.

GOING OUT

In the evening, people often go out for a stroll. They will meet with friends and family before dinner. Then they walk through the streets together. It is a time to see people and be seen yourself! Then it's time to eat.

FOOD AND DRINK

Food is an important part of Italian culture. People value home-cooked meals made from fresh ingredients. Breakfast is usually a simple meal. Children have hot chocolate with bread or pastry. Lunch is the main meal of the day. Many workers and students go home for lunch.

FAMOUS FOODS

Italy is known for its pasta. It is made from flour and water and, sometimes, eggs. It comes in many different shapes. Each has its own name. Pasta is usually served with sauce. Different regions in Italy have their own special sauces and pasta dishes.

Pizza is another famous Italian food. It has a base of flat dough with various toppings. The most traditional are tomato sauce, mozzarella cheese, and basil. For a sweet treat, Italians love gelato. It is a type of thick, creamy ice cream. It comes in many different flavors.

Panzanella goes well with other Italian food or can be eaten as a meal on its own.

PANZANELLA

This salad is a great way to use up stale bread. An Italian bread called ciabatta works well, but you can also use sourdough.

Panzanella Ingredients:
- 1 cup of stale bread
- 2 cups of ripe tomatoes
- 1 small red onion
- 6 tablespoons olive oil
- 2 tablespoons red wine vinegar
- salt and pepper
- fresh basil leaves

Panzanella Instructions:
1. Tear the bread into walnut-sized pieces and place on a tray to dry out.
2. Chop the tomatoes into similar-sized pieces. Put them in a bowl and season with salt and pepper.
3. Peel the onion and slice it very fine. Add it to the bowl with the tomatoes.
4. Add the dry bread, vinegar, and olive oil to the bowl and mix everything with your hands.
5. Tear up the basil leaves and sprinkle on top.

CHAPTER FIVE

HOLIDAYS AND CELEBRATIONS

More than 80 percent of Italians are Roman Catholic. Many of their festivals are Catholic too. Christmas is one of the most important. Italians set up nativity scenes. Children sometimes dress up as shepherds. Then they go caroling from house to house. On Christmas Eve, church bells ring at midnight.

Many children receive their gifts on January 6. The legend is that these presents are delivered by La Befana. She is an old woman who rides a broomstick. She fills socks with sweets and small presents.

People often dress as La Befana. Legend is she gives coal to naughty children.

CARNIVAL

The weeks before Easter are a time of prayer and fasting. Italians get ready for this by having a huge party beforehand! Each city has its own celebrations. The Venice **Carnival** is the most famous. People wear costumes and masks. There are balls and concerts. In the northern town of Ivrea, locals celebrate Carnival by having a food fight!

FERRAGOSTO

Italians celebrate Ferragosto on August 15. This is the day that Catholics believe Jesus's mother, Mary, rose into heaven. But Ferragosto is also based on an ancient Roman festival. Many people go to church. There are also parades and performances. For many people, it is the start of the summer holidays.

NATIONAL HOLIDAYS

Not all festivals in Italy are religious. On April 25, the country celebrates Liberation Day. It honors all Italians who died in World War II. May 1 is Labor Day. It is a chance to celebrate workers. Another holiday is the Festival of the Republic on June 2. It celebrates Italy becoming a republic in 1946.

A statue of the Virgin Mary is carried through the streets for Ferragosto.

Tens of thousands of spectators crowd into the main square to watch the Palio.

THE PALIO

In the city of Siena, Ferragosto is celebrated with a horse race called the Palio. Ten of the city's districts enter a horse and rider. After a parade, the jockeys ride bareback around the town square. They do three laps. The race is over in about 90 seconds. The first horse to cross the finish line wins, even if the jockey has fallen off!

CHAPTER SIX

SPORTS AND RECREATION

Soccer is the most popular sport in Italy. Italians call it *calcio*, which means "kick." Huge crowds watch the top professional teams play. Some teams, such as Juventus and AC Milan, have won European competitions. Italians also support their country's national team. They have won the World Cup four times. Only Brazil has won it more.

The Italian soccer team is known as the "Azzurri," which means "the Blues."

CYCLING AND BASKETBALL

In May, Italians line the roads throughout the country. They have come to watch a bicycle race. The world's top riders compete in the Giro d'Italia. It lasts for three weeks. The race's route changes every year. It is usually about 2,200 miles (3,500 km) long!

Many people in Italy play basketball. There are clubs and amateur teams. There is also a professional league. The men's national team has won silver twice at the Olympics.

MOTOR RACING

Italy is also famous for motor racing. Ferrari is an Italian company. It has built some of the world's best racing cars. Italian drivers have won many races. Valentino Rossi is one of the world's top motorcycle racers.

OTHER SPORTS

Fencing has always been popular in Italy. Its national team has won more Olympic medals than any other country. Rugby is also popular, especially in the north. Since 2000, Italy has competed in the Six Nations tournament. This is a rugby competition between the nations of England, Ireland, Scotland, Wales, France, and Italy.

Italy's mountains have many ski resorts. People go to the Alps on skiing holidays. Top skiers compete in races. From snowy slopes to ancient sites, Italy has something for everyone.

FACT

Fencer Valentina Vezzali has won nine Olympic medals—six of them gold! Her success made her a celebrity in Italy. In 2013, she was elected to the Italian parliament.

Many Italian families enjoy skiing together in the Alps.

PIOVRA

Piovra is a traditional Italian children's game. Its name is the Italian word for octopus. One player pretends to be an octopus and catches the others in his or her "tentacles." You can play with 5 to 12 people.

1. Choose one person to be the octopus. The others should all go to one end of the field or playground.
2. At the same time, all the players try to run past the octopus and reach the opposite side. The octopus is only allowed to move from side to side, not forward or backward.
3. Anyone who is tagged has to freeze. They are now a baby octopus. They stand in one place and swing their arms to catch runners.
4. The game is over when all the children have been captured.

GLOSSARY

Allies (AL-eyes)
the countries that fought with Britain and the United States in World Wars I and II

canal (ku-NAL)
an artificial channel of water built to let ships travel on it

Carnival (CAR-ni-vul)
a celebration that happens immediately before the period of prayer and fasting known as Lent

city-state (SIT-ee STAYT)
a city and the lands surrounding it, which are independent and not part of a larger country

empire (EM-pire)
a large area of land ruled over by a single person or group

European Union (YOO-ro-PEE-un YOON-yun)
a political organization of countries in Europe that work together on trade and other issues

gladiator (GLAD-ee-ay-tur)
a person in ancient Rome who was trained to fight against other gladiators or animals for entertainment

independent (in-de-PEN-duhnt)
not ruled over by anyone else

peninsula (puh-NIN-suh-luh)
a piece of land that juts out into a body of water

republic (ri-PUB-lick)
a state that is run by elected officials rather than by a king or queen

volcano (vol-KAY-no)
a mountain with a crater at the top, through which lava, gas, and ash can erupt

READ MORE

Challen, Paul. *The Culture and Crafts of Italy*.
New York: PowerKids Press, 2016.

Kelly, Tracey. *The Culture and Recipes of Italy*.
New York: Rosen, 2017.

Vonne, Mira. *Gross Facts About the Roman Empire*.
Mankato, MN: Capstone, 2017.

INTERNET SITES

Discover Italy
italia.it/en/home.html

Encyclopedia Britannica: Fast Facts about Italy
britannica.com/place/Italy

Science for Kids: Colosseum Facts
www.scienceforkidsclub.com/colosseum.html

INDEX

OTHER BOOKS IN THIS SERIES